GEHAZI
THE SINNER DETECTED

"These things were our examples, to the intent that we should not lust after evil things as they also lusted."
1 Corinthians 10:6

Gehazi

The Sinner Detected

A Sermon–*in Puritan style*–on Temptation
and Secret Sins: "Be sure your sin will
find you out." *Numbers 32*

2010 Illustrated Edition

Newly Modernized, Revised, and
Expanded *from D. P. Kidder's 1848
Sunday School Edition*

Hail & Fire
www.hailandfire.com

"Gehazi, or, The Sinner Detected," revised by
D. P. Kidder, 1848 Sunday School Edition, is
herein newly modernized, revised, and
expanded by Hail & Fire.

ISBN-10 0982804318
ISBN-13 978-0-9828043-1-5

Hail & Fire is a resource for Reformed and
Gospel Theology in the works, exhortations,
prayers, and apologetics of those who have
maintained the Gospel and expounded upon
the Scripture as the Eternal Word of God and
the sole authority in Christian doctrine.

Visit us online at: www.hailandfire.com

*For the admonition of all
and the strengthening
of God's elect*

CONTENTS

ILLUSTRATIONS

"By manifestation of the truth commending
ourselves to every man's conscience
in the sight of God."
2 Corinthians 3:2

HAIL & FIRE
Reprints and Republications

Hail & Fire is a resource for Reformed and Gospel Theology in the works, exhortations, prayers, and apologetics of those who have maintained the Gospel and expounded upon the Scripture as the Eternal Word of God and the sole authority in Christian doctrine.

For the edification of those who believe the Gospel in truth and for the examination of all consciences, Hail & Fire reprints and republishes, in print and online, Christian, Puritan, Reformed and Protestant sermons and exhortative works; Protestant and Catholic polemical and apologetical works; Bibles, histories, martyrologies, and eschatological works.

Visit us online at:
www.hailandfire.com

"These words which I command you this day shall be in your heart and you shall diligently teach them to your children."
Deuteronomy 6:6-7

PREFACE
To the Christian Teacher

"You that are parents, or to whom the education of children is committed, I beseech you to mind how great a duty lies upon you. ... For to what purpose do we desire them before we have them, rejoice in them when we have them, value them so highly, sympathize with them so tenderly, grieve for their death so excessively, if in the meantime no care be taken what shall become of them to eternity?"

"If you neglect to instruct them in the way of holiness, will the devil neglect to instruct them in the way of wickedness? No, if you will not teach them to pray, he will teach them to curse, swear and lie."

"There is none in the world so likely as you to be instruments of their eternal good. You have peculiar advantages that no one else has."

"The consideration of the great day, should move your bowels of pity for them. Oh remember that text (Revelation 20:12) 'I saw the dead, small and great, stand before God.' What a sad thing will it be to see your dear children at Christ's left hand! Oh friends! Do your utmost to prevent this misery! 'Knowing the terrors of the Lord, we persuade men.' (2 Corinthians 5:11)"

John Flavel
1627-1691, Puritan Preacher
(Divine Conduct, or, The Mystery of Providence)

"Christian children mainly need to be taught the doctrine, precept, and life of the gospel: they require to have Divine truth put before them clearly and forcibly. ... If there be any doctrine too difficult for a child, it is rather the fault of [our] conception of it than of the child's power to receive it, provided that child be really converted to God. It is ours to make doctrine simple; this is to be a main part of our work. Teach the little ones the whole truth and nothing but the truth; for instruction is the great want of the child's nature. ... Children in grace have to grow, rising to greater capacity in knowing, being, doing, and feeling, and to greater power from God; therefore above all things they must be fed. ... Whether we teach young Christians truth or not, the devil will be sure to teach them error. ... The more the young are taught the better—it will keep them from being misled."

"We are especially exhorted to feed them because they are so likely to be overlooked. I am afraid our sermons often go over the heads of the younger folk - who, nevertheless, may be as true Christians as the older ones. Blessed is he who can so speak as to be understood by a child!"

Charles H. Spurgeon
1834-1892 Baptist Preacher
(Come Ye Children)

GEHAZI
The Sinner Detected

You must have often noticed that people, both children and those who are grown up, will do many things when they think they are not seen, that they would not do if they knew they were being watched. Surely you have known children who were very well behaved in school while the teacher was present, but who behaved very badly when any situation required the teacher to be absent. Indeed, have you not seen and felt something like this in yourself? Have you not been tempted to do something that you knew was wrong? Perhaps you looked around, and seeing no one, you thought, 'I can do this and get away with it, because nobody will see me.' Then suddenly, just at that very moment, you caught sight of someone—'My dad is coming' or, 'I see my mom.' You were going to give into an evil temptation, but you were stopped when you realized, 'If I do this I will surely be seen and punished.'

But now I want you to remember that you are never actually alone. There is an eye that is always watching you.[1] In the thirty-second chapter of the Bible's book of Numbers[2] you will find that after wandering a long time in the wilderness, the Israelite people had come to the borders of the land of Canaan. When they were about to enter in to take possession of the Promise Land the tribes of Reuben and Gad asked to stay and have their inheritance in the land they were already in, instead of crossing over the Jordan River. At first Moses believed their request had come from bad motives, and he told them so. But after they had explained the matter just so, he was satisfied, but strongly warned them to keep their promise. He reminded them that if they did not, they would not escape their punishment. His warning was given in very serious and solemn words, and I want you to take special note of them. You can find them

1. "The eyes of the LORD are in every place, keeping watch on the evil and the good." Proverbs 15:3

2. Numbers 32

in the twenty-third verse of the chapter. He tells the people who were standing before him, that if they do not keep their promise, not only would they injure their brethren, but they would commit a sin against God. He also tells them that God, whom they would be sinning against, would not allow them to escape, but would certainly punish them. Look at the words he uses: *"If you do not do so, behold, you have sinned against the Lord; and you may be sure that your sin will find you out."*[3]

Yes, whenever we do wrong we sin against God; and sooner or later, in one way or another, our sin will find us out. There is no pardoning of sin without repentance; and the sorrows of repentance are only produced by remembering and regretting past sin. If we do not allow our sins to find us out in this way, so that we are truly ashamed of them and turn away from doing them again, then our sins will find us out in their punishment. Never forget this truth. Whenever you are tempted

---

3. Numbers 32:23

to sin, remember the prophetic voice warning you:

"YOUR SIN WILL FIND YOU OUT"

In order to impress this truth more deeply into your mind, or rather, to plant it into your innermost soul, I am going to direct your attention to a remarkable story found in the fifth chapter of the Bible's Second Book of Kings.[4] The story tells us about Gehazi, the servant of the prophet Elisha.

You may read the whole chapter:

> "Now Naaman, commander of the army of the king of Syria, was a great and honorable man in his master's eyes, because through him the Lord had given Syria victory. He was also a mighty man of valor, but he was a leper.[5]
>
> And the Syrians had gone out on raids, and had brought back captive a young girl from the land of Israel; and she waited on Naaman's wife.

4. 2 Kings 5
5. A person with a skin disease called Leprosy.

[4]

The young Israelite girl tells her mistress that the prophet Elisha could heal Naaman of his leprosy.

And she said to her mistress, 'If only my lord were with the prophet that is in Samaria! For he would heal him of his leprosy.'

And Naaman went and told his master, saying, 'Thus and thus said the girl that is from the land of Israel.'

And the king of Syria said, 'Go and I will send a letter to the king of Israel.' And he departed, and took with him ten talents of silver, and six thousand pieces of gold, and ten changes of clothing.

And he brought the letter to the king of Israel, which said, 'Now when this letter comes to you, behold, I have sent Naaman my servant to you, that you may heal him of his leprosy.'

And it came to pass, when the king of Israel had read the letter, that he tore his clothes, and said, 'Am I God, that I can kill and make alive, that this man sends a man to me to be healed of his leprosy? Therefore please consider, and see how he seeks to quarrel with me.'

And it was so, when Elisha the man of God had heard that the king of Israel had torn his clothes, that he sent to the king, saying, 'Why have you torn your clothes? let him now come to me, and he will know that there is a prophet in Israel.'

So Naaman came with his horses and with his chariot, and stood at the door of the house of Elisha.

And Elisha sent a messenger to him, saying, 'Go and wash in the Jordan River seven times, and your flesh will be restored to you, and you will be clean.'

But Naaman was angry and went away, and said, 'Behold, I thought, He will surely come out to me, and stand and call on the name of the Lord his God, and strike his hand over the place and heal the leprosy.

Are not Abanah and Pharpar, the rivers of Damascus, better than all the waters of Israel? Could I not wash in them and be clean?' So he turned and went away in a rage.

And his servants came near, and spoke to him, and said, 'My father, if the prophet had told you to do something great, would you not have done it? How much more then when he says to you, Wash and be clean?'

Then he went down and dipped himself seven times in the Jordan, according to what the man of God has said. His flesh was restored like the flesh of a little child, and he was clean.

And he returned to the man of God, him and all his company, and came and stood before him, and he said, 'Behold, now I know that there is no God in all the earth, but in Israel. Now therefore, please take a gift from your servant.'

But he said, 'As the Lord lives, before whom I stand, I will take nothing.' And he urged him to take it, but he refused.

And Naaman said, 'Then please let two mule loads of earth be given to your servant; for your servant will not offer either burnt offering or sacrifice to other gods, but to the Lord only.

Naaman is completely healed of his leprosy when he
obeys the instructions of the prophet Elisha and dips
himself seven times in the Jordan.

In this one thing may the Lord pardon your servant, that when my master goes into the temple of Rimmon to worship there, and he leans on my hand, and I bow myself in the temple of Rimmon: when I bow down myself in the house of Rimmon, may the Lord pardon your servant in this thing.'

And he said to him, 'Go in peace.' So he departed from him a little distance.

But Gehazi, the servant of Elisha, the man of God, said, 'Behold, my master has spared Naaman, this Syrian, in not taking from his hand what he brought; but, as the LORD lives, I will run after him and take something from him.'

So Gehazi followed after Naaman and when Naaman saw him running after him, he got down from the chariot to meet him, and said, 'Is all well?'

And he said, 'All is well. My master has sent me, saying, "Behold, just now two young men of the sons of the prophets have come to me from Mount Ephraim: please give them a talent of silver and two changes of clothing."'

Gehazi lies to Naaman in order to get some of
the gifts the prophet Elisha had refused.

And Naaman said, 'Please, take two talents.' And he urged him, and bound two talents of silver in two bags, with two changes of clothing, and he gave them to two of his servants; and they carried them on ahead of him.

And when he came to the tower, he took them from their hand and stored them in the house: and he let the men go, and they departed.

Then he went in and stood before his master. And Elisha said to him, 'Where have you come from, Gehazi?' And he said, 'Your servant went nowhere.'

And he said to him, 'Did my heart not go with you, when the man turned back from his chariot to meet you? Is it time to receive money, and to receive clothing, and oliveyards and vineyards, and sheep and oxen, and menservants and maidservants?

Therefore, the leprosy of Naaman will cling to you and to your descendants forever.' And he went out from his presence a leper, as white as snow."

Gehazi's sin is exposed by the prophet Elisha.

In the first part of the chapter we read that very interesting account of the young servant girl who was taken captive from the land of Israel and waited on the wife of Naaman. We read that Naaman was a great and powerful commander, who was highly honored by his master the king of Syria, and how he was miraculously cured of his leprosy by obeying the instructions of God's prophet Elisha. But, it is at the last eight verses of the chapter that I want you to really focus on right now. This is where we read about the evil behavior of Elisha's servant Gehazi.

It seems that when Naaman came out of the water completely cured of his disease, he wanted to express how grateful he was by giving the prophet a generous gift. But Elisha refused to accept any present at all. He knew that the miracle had not been done by him, but by God. He wanted to show this man how different the only true religion was from those that were practiced in countries outside the land of Israel. For, up until this moment, Naaman had been a heathen and was only familiar with the heathen priests—who were seldom anything more than impostors. He wanted to show him that he did not seek his own honor or promotion. So, although Naaman urged him, he continued to refuse the gift and would not take anything from him. Elisha's refusal was intended to strengthen the impression that the miracle had just made and to win over the respect and homage of Naaman's feelings, his faith, and his way of life, to the truth.

Now we come to the fearful lesson to be learned from the story. Naaman had left the home of the prophet and was returning to his own land. He was happy in his restored health, and must have been thoughtfully considering all the things that he had been shown by these events—such as his amazing cure, the vast consequences of the existence of the only true God, and that new religious character Elisha's disinterest in rewards had shown to him—when suddenly he was interrupted by the approach of Gehazi to his chariot.

Gehazi had heard Naaman's offer of gifts to Elisha. He had most likely seen that some of this Syrian general's servants were carrying the sort of things with them that would have been good to give if the offer had been accepted. He looked and he coveted those objects. We do not know whether he wanted those possessions for himself only (just as many people want to own the things they believe are signs of wealth—such as money, land, and houses—just for the sake of knowing they own them and because they have them they are rich), or if he wanted the possessions for his family sake, so that he could give them wealth as his successors and heirs. The punishment for his sin seems almost to indicate this when it says: *The leprosy will cling to you and to your descendants forever,"* verse 27. But whatever his motives were, it is beyond all doubt that he had a covetous desire, which was the starting point of his evil actions.

In this example we can see how all evil actions begin. It was in this very same manner that sin first entered the world. The devil presented the forbidden fruit as an object to be desired. At first the temptation was only external and no sin had been committed. The desire could have been ignored and refused. Eve could have said, 'I will not even look at something that must be wrong—because God has forbidden it.' But instead, she allowed the desire to take hold of her until she had fixed her heart upon tasting the forbidden fruit. She immediately entered into temptation and by doing this, let in the seed of all sins.

For this reason the Apostle Peter teaches us that *"the corruption which is in the world"* is here *"through lust,"*[6] that is, through desire for things that are forbidden. As long as we carefully watch over and guard our desires, we are safe. If we fix our desire on good and right things and turn away from bad and evil things, no evil can overtake us. Things that are outside of us cannot actually make us sin—this inclination or movement must come from within us. For this reason God's law commands us, *"You shall not covet."*[7] But when restraint and self-control are overcome by evil desire and a sinful thing is allowed to take root within us, then the power and influence of temptation begins. *"Every man is tempted when he is drawn away by his own lust, and enticed."*[8] These words are extremely

---

6. 2 Peter 1:4   8. James 1:14
7. Deuteronomy 5:21

important. A fisherman baits his hook, the hook is attached to his fishing line, the line to his fishing pole, but the fish is not actually drawn out of the water until it willingly takes the bait itself. In this very same way, our own desires and lusts allow Satan—that wicked fisher for souls—to trick us into sinning because we have willingly permitted ourselves to be lured by his bait. Therefore, guard against those first consenting inclinations of your heart. Watch out for them and keep a firm hold on them. Satan has no power over you except in this way—when your heart willingly agrees to his temptations and gives into them. It is not merely the bait being offered on the hook that gives the fish to the fisherman, but it is the bait being willingly taken into the fish's mouth. Just the same, it is not merely the outward temptation shown to our mind that causes us to sin, but rather, it is us allowing the outward temptation to create a desire within us. *"Every man is tempted when he is drawn away by his own lust,"* that is, improper desire.

Let us look again at Gehazi. He wants to possess the gift Naaman offered to his master. God, the Searcher of hearts, has given this to us as an example of the immediate consequences of allowing an evil desire to take root. *"Gehazi, the servant of Elisha, the man of God, said, 'Behold, my master has spared Naaman, this Syrian, in not taking from his hand what he brought; but, as the LORD lives, I will run after him and take something from him,'"* verse 20. Here is the first step in the progress of sin—a resolution to commit it. Allowing the desire was sinful; but still the sinful act had not yet been committed. The desire could have been extinguished.[9] It is true, however, that when the mind has already been permitted to go this far, it is difficult to stop it. It is easier to refuse the bait than it is to remove it. There is now a power from outside working upon the soul. Still, although the task is difficult, it is not impossible. By immediately praying to God's for His help and intervention and showing sincerity by a determined resistance to the inward sin that has already begun, it may be overcome and escaped from. The

9. "God is faithful, who will not allow you to be tempted beyond what you are able, but with the temptation will also make a way to escape." 1 Corinthians 10:13.

danger is imminent and the peril is fearful. There is not a moment to be lost. What is to be done for escape must be done decidedly and at once.

Gehazi, however, put up no fight whatsoever. On the contrary, he completely relished the desire. He had considered the matter and his choice was enthusiastic and entire. His words show this. He even appeals on the subject to God, against whom he was sinning, by saying *"As the Lord lives, I will run after him, and take something from him," verse 20.*

And now the sinful act begins—*"So Gehazi followed after Naaman,"* verse 21. Temptation had called his attention to a forbidden object. Instead of resisting, he gave into it and permitted the evil desire to take root; and loving it, he went on to commit the evil act. He left the house, and taking the right road, he soon caught up with the chariot in which the Syrian captain was slowly returning home— meditating, no doubt, on the wonderful things that had taken place. On his way, Gehazi had time to concoct his whole plan; and as soon as he caught up with Naaman he put it into action. He did not dare to say that his master had changed his mind; instead, he invented a tale which he thought would be enough to convince Naaman, and shield himself. His approach was noticed, *"and when Naaman saw him running after him, he got down from his chariot to meet him."* His respect for the master clearly extended to the servant as well. Not knowing if something might have happened he asked, *"Is all well?"* And now we see again the progress of sin—one sin leads to another. To obtain his goal a lie was necessary; and with a direct lie Gehazi—this professed worshiper of the God of truth—was well prepared. He answered, *"All is well. My master has sent me, saying, 'Behold, just now two young men of the sons of the prophets have come to me from Mount Ephraim: please give them a talent of silver and two changes of clothing,'"* verse 22. Naaman did not suspect any mischief and was obviously glad to be allowed to show his appreciation. Therefore, he gave him even more than he had asked for. *"And Naaman said, 'Please, take two talents.' And he urged him, and bound two talents of silver in two bags, with two changes of clothing, and he gave them to two of his servants; and they carried them on ahead of him,"* verse 23.

The sin was now complete. This is the natural order in which sin progresses. When temptation attacks us and we do not resist it, but instead receive it willingly, it becomes a sinful desire. We have already sinned in our heart. But when sin is permitted to stay in the heart, it will most certainly, as far as there is opportunity, influence and affect our conduct and there will be a sinful act and the outright breaking of God's law. Rarely is this found to end with just one sinful incident. Having begun to sin, we shall find it necessary to go on sinning—adding sin to sin—just as Gehazi added lying to his covetous resolution to get what he had no right to have. No one can tell, when he begins to sin, just how far he will go before he can stop. There is no safety except to decidedly resist a temptation at its very start. It will not be difficult to put out the spark while it is only a spark—otherwise, *"behold how great a fire a little spark kindles!"*[10]

10. James 3:5

Gehazi, having accomplished his plan, now thought about how he could make his prize safe. Naaman's servants helped him to carry everything home: *"and they carried them on ahead of him. And when he came to the tower,"* the place where Elisha lived, *"he took them from their hand, and stored them in the house: and he let the men go, and they departed,"* verse 24.

Having now hidden what he had so unjustly acquired, he thought that all was safe. His conscience had been asleep all this time and he was, no doubt, congratulating himself on his success and looking at himself as a much richer man than he had ever been. He would likely try to convince himself that he had done the right thing. When we look at any action, we have the ability to look at it from whatever point of view we choose to. In what he had done, Gehazi wanted to see an act by which he appeared to be a great winner. He saw the two talents of silver and the two changes of clothing, but he would not look at the moral nature of his actions. He did not stop to consider in what relationship to God his act had placed him. He saw that he was a richer man, but he refused to see that he was also a guilty man. We should never be content until we have looked at our behavior in its moral light. It may be successful in helping our present earthly condition—and many people are so blinded by and happy with this that they look no further—but we should always first ask how it will affect our spiritual condition. We should ask whether the action is good or evil in God's eyes and how the action appears when we weigh and test it by the perfect standard of His holy law.

Up until this point, Gehazi had found that everything was going well for him and having safely secured the property that he had unlawfully gained, he went back to his usual attendance upon Elisha—unaware of what awaited him. *"He went in, and stood before his master."* The first words which were spoken to him could scarcely have failed to disturb his false happiness: *"Elisha said to him, 'Where have you come from, Gehazi?'"* It was not to be expected that after doing what he had done, he would honestly confess his fault and beg for forgiveness. So he went on and added to his guilt another lie. Sin leads to sin and one sin draws another after it. He replied—but surely with some inward fear and hesitation—*"Your servant went nowhere."*

And now comes the detection of sin. What would his confusion and shame be when he heard these words from one whom he knew was a prophet of the Most High?—*"And [Elisha] said to him, 'Did my heart not go with you, when the man turned back from his chariot to meet you? Is it time to receive money, and to receive clothing, and oliveyards and vineyards, and sheep and oxen, and menservants and maidservants?'"* In his dreams of the future, Gehazi probably thought of what he might become by using the property he had sinfully gotten. He must have imagined his future advancement in the world and seen himself as an owner of oliveyards and vineyards, waited upon by many menservants and maidservants, who would help him take care of his herds of oxen and flocks of sheep. Visions of prosperity must have stretched out before his imagination. But the prophet spoke and the sinner felt that his sin was known. He awoke from his dream. The vision passed away, along with all the pleasure he had thinking about it. Nothing remained but the guilt with all its pain and bitter shame. For a little while sin had been sweet to him, but the sweetness was now gone forever and lasting bitterness took its place.

Sooner or later it will always turn out this way. However secretly we sin, there is always an eye that sees everything we do. People may not see us, but God sees us. In the wonderful order of His almighty providence He may cause the detection of our sin to take place in this world. He may so expose us in front of people that, of all our schemes, successful as we thought they were, nothing remains but the sin. As pleasant as the fruit we took from the forbidden tree was, the pleasure passes away and nothing remains but the painful and humiliating sense of guilt. But even if this is not our case in this life, nothing will stop it from taking place as soon as we die and leave this world. We leave the profits and pleasures of sin behind, but we take our sin and its guilt along with us forever. As soon as we are *"absent from the body,"* we are *"present with the Lord."*[11]; and we will find ourselves standing before, not some Elisha, but Elisha's

God. We will stand before our Judge; and we will stand before Him as we really are. *"All things are naked and open to the eyes of Him to whom we must give an account."* Never forget this. *"There is no creature that is hidden from His sight."*[12] He knows us now and He will make us to know ourselves then. However blind and hardened a sinner may be, as soon as he stands before God, in that awful moment his sin is completely exposed, his conscience wakes up, and the gnawing of that 'worm which never dies' begins.[13]

But being exposed is not the end of it. Punishment follows immediately. Let us now look at the fearful conclusion of the prophet's words to Gehazi: *"Therefore, the leprosy of Naaman will cling to you, and to your descendants forever."* He had meant to increase his wealth and establish his family by sinning against God; but instead, he had brought down on himself and his family this terrible disease—for God's word was not given in vain. Elisha was only the instrument

11. 2 Corinthians 5:8   13. Isaiah 66:24; Mark 9:48
12. Hebrews 4:13

used to speak the sentence of God. Therefore, infliction of the actual punishment followed immediately. As the exposed sinner listened, he could feel the disease running through his veins and taking hold of his whole body. He could look at his hands and see the frightening proof that his punishment had taken place. He had come before his master self-satisfied, congratulating himself on the success of his fraud, but he departed from him, condemned and punished: *"And he went out from his presence a leper, as white as snow,"* verse 27.

Sometimes sin is punished in this world, but whether or not this is the case, it will most certainly be punished in the world to come. Whoever does not repent and turn away from his sins while he is alive, will die in the guilt of them and he will *"lift up his eyes in hell, being in torments."*[14] On the last day when he stands before the judgment seat of Jesus Christ, he will hear the dreadful words of the sentence that will be carried out immediately:

14. Luke 16:23

"Depart from Me, you cursed, into everlasting fire, prepared for the devil and his angels!"[15]

And when the wicked have, in this manner, "gone away into everlasting punishment," what will it have profited them that in their lifetime they received their good things?[16] Supposing they had gained the whole world, they have lost their own souls.[17] The earthly gain is gone and the pleasure is all over, but the perdition remains and will remain forever: *"Their worm does not die, and their fire is not quenched."*[18]

In this way, the example of Gehazi illustrates for us the whole history of sin—its beginning and origin, its progress and completion, its detection and punishment.

Does all of this not show us the amazing foolishness of sin? We cannot trick God.[19] We cannot hide anything from Him; we cannot resist His set times for judgment. We may disobey His laws, but we cannot in any way

---

15. Matthew 25:41   17. Mark 8:36

16. Luke 16:25   18. Isaiah 66:24

19. "Do not be deceived, God is not mocked. For

keep Him from carrying out the sentence He pronounces against the disobedient. Even while the punishment is delayed, the sentence hangs over us. We are condemned already and cannot really be happy in sin. The handwriting is already on the wall against us,[20] and if we do not see it, it is only because we will not lift up our eyes to look at it. We have nothing more than the false peace of stubborn and willful ignorance. This pretend peace is always subject to interruption and at the very longest can only last though our lifetime. It is over as soon as we die and it leaves us forever. Nothing will remain then but the bitter consequences of wrongdoing—guilt, shame, misery, and utter despair—for all eternity and without any more opportunities to repent and be forgiven.

What lessons should we learn then from this history?

First: We must secure the good favor of God and with that we will have true peace

whatever a man sows, that he will also reap."
Galatians 6:7

20. Daniel 5

of conscience. "Repent therefore, and be converted that your sins may blotted out," Acts 3:19. The good favor of God is secured through the forgiveness of our sins by faith in the atoning death of Jesus Christ on the cross, who "died once for all," Hebrews 10:10. And that faith is a lively faith, which cleanses and sanctifies us—governing our every action and our every thought in holiness. "Let us draw near with a true heart in the full assurance of faith, having our hearts sprinkled from an evil conscience and our bodies washed with pure water," Hebrews 10:22. Let us "Go and sin no more," John 8:11. We wish to be happy and this is the only way to be happy. "Therefore submit yourselves to God. Resist the devil and he will flee from you," James 4:7. In this way God becomes our Father and our Friend. While we live, He will guide us with His counsel, and when we die, He will receive us into His glory.

Second: We must never dally or fool around with temptation, but fully resist it at once. Do not look at the talents of silver and the changes of clothing only, but at the leprosy also. Do not be content with asking what instant gain will this action get me? Also ask, what relationship does it have to the law of God? The tempter points only to the seeming advantages of an evil action, but look at its moral character. It may be pleasurable or profitable for a moment, but is it right? Depend upon this: sin is always a losing matter and sooner or later you will find it to be so. Therefore, do not have anything to do with sin. Resist the temptation as soon as it is presented to you. Do not allow yourself to desire anything that can only be had by sinning against God. Let it be a set rule and principle for you: "Whether I gain or lose, I must not sin. Whatever I seek, I must seek it only in the paths of righteousness. I must not leave the way to heaven and enter the way to hell to find it. Talents of silver and changes of clothing may be useful for mere earthly comfort, but the favor of God is absolutely necessary, both for my earthly happiness and my eternal well being."

The young especially should remember these things. Their life is ahead of them, and it is most important that they start out right. There is the providence of God, as well as the final judgment of God. The tempter often tries to trick young people into beginning life by only looking at the talents of silver and the changes of clothing. He tries to trick them into seeking these things in ways that practically set aside the authority and claims of God. Let everyone who is tempted in this way think of what the consequences might be. Let them remember Gehazi with his gains *and* with his leprosy, and let them be wise in time. Seeming earthly advantages may be connected to heavy crosses and bitter trials all the way through life, even though the sin may be pardoned and the soul put in safety. Depend upon this truth—true wisdom exists only in obeying the direction of our Lord, *"Seek the kingdom of God first and His righteousness, and all other things will be added to you."*[21]

In every situation, no matter what may come from it, never allow yourself to even wish for something you cannot have consistently with the will of God. As soon as any temptation comes upon you, say with the martyr who was offered life if he would deny Jesus, *"None*

21. Matthew 6:33

but Christ! none but Christ!"[22] The tempter may point to the talents of silver, and the changes of clothing, but look beyond them to the leprosy which they will bring. Yes, if you are ever tempted to sin like Gehazi, let the memory of Gehazi's punishment rebuke you. Never forget the solemn words of Jesus Christ, your Savior and your Judge, *"What will it profit a man, if he gains the whole world, and loses his own soul?"*[23]

To sum up the whole matter in a few words: Gehazi began by allowing himself to desire something he knew he could not have in accordance with the will of God; he permitted and loved the desire and it led to his direct and repeated acts of sin. For a short time this appeared to have been successful for him, but it was only for a short time. His sin was detected and exposed, and his punishment immediately followed. Therefore, whenever

22. The Christian martyr John Lambert, a Protestant, was condemned as a heretic by the Roman Catholic Church and burned alive at the stake in 1538 for his faith in the Gospel of Jesus Christ.

23. Matthew 16:26

you are tempted to sin, think hard about Gehazi and his leprosy.

THE END

"Let no man deceive you with vain words: for because of these things the wrath of God comes upon the children of disobedience."
Ephesians 5:6

"Be zealous and repent."
Revelation 3:19

"Submit yourselves to God. Resist the devil and he will flee from you."
James 4:7

www.ingramcontent.com/pod-product-compliance
Lightning Source LLC
Chambersburg PA
CBHW060723030426
42337CB00017B/2981